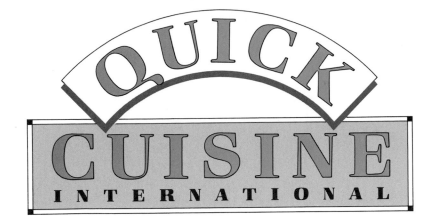

QUICK CUISINE INTERNATIONAL

New Recipes for
Italian Favorites

THE KNAPP PRESS

PUBLISHERS
LOS ANGELES

Published by The Knapp Press
5900 Wilshire Boulevard, Los Angeles, California 90036

Library of Congress Cataloging in Publication Data

Main entry under title:
New recipes for Italian favorites
(Quick cuisine international)
Includes index
1. Cookery, Italian.   I. Series.
TX723.N49   1984   641.5945   84–14402
ISBN 0–89535–147–1

On the cover: *Antipasto Salad*
Recipes developed by Naomi Shuwarger
Cover photograph: Teri Sandison
Food stylist: Jean E. Carey
Food styling assistant: Sandy Krogh

Printed and bound in the United States of America
10   9   8   7   6   5   4   3   2   1

Contents

Introduction

For me, the pleasures of good food combined with the spirited company of family and friends is essential to living well. Family meals filled with lively conversation and wonderful Italian dishes, lovingly prepared, are some of my happiest memories. The demands of my everyday life, however, make it impossible for me to devote the hours to meal preparation that my mother and grandmother accepted as part of their daily routine. So, in order to have the best of both worlds—a busy contemporary lifestyle with the quality of old-world traditions—I've collected my favorite family recipes and adapted them to meet the requirements of my busy schedule. My goal in altering these recipes was to shorten the preparation and cooking time, yet still achieve results as good as those produced by hours over a hot stove.

With my approach to authentic Italian cooking, zesty Spinach Stracciatella Soup (page 31) is ready to serve in only twenty minutes; Turkey Breasts Marsala (page 75) in only twenty-five. Even a delicious, impromptu dinner party becomes possible after a hectic day. Just pick up a crusty loaf of Italian bread and a chilled bottle of white Chianti or Soave on the way home and prepare Tomato, Buffalo Mozzarella, and Basil Salad (page 11), Pasta with Smoked Salmon and Golden Caviar (page 39), and, perhaps, Fruit Cioccolata (page 111) for a spectacular dessert. As you browse through the beautiful, full-color photographs that show imaginative ways to present each dish, I hope you'll find inspiration for a variety of great, quick menus.

This book was a joy to create. I found myself reliving great meals with my mother and grandmother as they helped me find quicker ways to prepare their delicious, traditional dishes. And, in the process, I got all sorts of new ideas for quick and creative meal planning. I hope *New Recipes for Italian Favorites* offers you the same inspiration and—most of all—gives you the time to lead your busy life without giving up the pleasure of cooking at home with imagination and style.

—*Anna Maria Victor*

*" . . . traditional ingredients in a
contemporary salad . . . simple, light
and delicious."*

Tomato, Buffalo Mozzarella and Fresh Basil Salad

6 servings

1 cup loosely packed fresh
   basil leaves
3 small garlic cloves
⅓ cup pine nuts, toasted (toast
   10 minutes at 350°F)
½ cup grated Parmesan cheese
½ cup olive oil
   Salt and pepper to taste
6 large ripe tomatoes, sliced to
   medium thickness
   Red-leaf lettuce
10 ounces buffalo mozzarella
   cheese, cut into ¼-inch dice

1 With a mortar and pestle or a processor, crush basil, garlic, pine nuts and Parmesan cheese with olive oil, making a paste. Add salt and pepper.

2 On a large serving platter, arrange tomato slices in an overlapping layer on a bed of red-leaf lettuce in the following manner: Arrange 1 slice tomato with a thin layer of basil sauce on top, and dot with dice of mozzarella. Continue layering ingredients in the same order, ending with the mozzarella dice.

*"This salad is probably my favorite. The
dressing is great."*

Chopped Salad with Parmesan Dressing

6 to 8 servings

½ **head iceberg lettuce, chopped into medium pieces**
1 **small head romaine lettuce, chopped**
¼ **pound Italian salami, finely diced**
¼ **pound mozzarella cheese, finely chopped**
1 **cup garbanzo beans (chickpeas), drained, rinsed and chopped**

Parmesan Dressing

Makes ½ cup

5 **tablespoons vegetable oil**
2 **tablespoons white wine vinegar**
1 **teaspoon dry mustard**
1 **teaspoon salt**
½ **teaspoon pepper**
½ **cup grated Parmesan cheese**

1 Combine all salad ingredients in a bowl.

2 Pour Parmesan Dressing over salad and toss, coating ingredients completely. Serve immediately.

1 Combine all ingredients in a jar with tight-fitting lid and shake well.

"...my father's favorite and now my husband's as well."

Roasted Peppers and Anchovies in Garlic Oil

6 servings

6 red bell peppers
6 garlic cloves, peeled, cut into fourths and crushed
1 2-ounce can flat anchovy fillets
Pepper to taste
¾ cup olive oil

1 Place peppers on a foil-lined baking sheet under broiler. As tops blacken and blister, turn until all sides are done. Remove and immediately place in a plastic bag and seal; let stand 15 minutes. (*They will steam in the bag and be easier to peel.*)

2 Peel peppers, remove tops and ribs from insides, and cut into strips 1 to 1½ inches in width.

3 Layer ingredients in a small, deep rectangular or square glass or enamel container in the following order: peppers, garlic, anchovies and pepper. Repeat until they are used up. Pour olive oil over all. Marinate in refrigerator from 2 hours to several days.

If you wish to serve this the same day, marinate it at room temperature for as long as possible. You may remove the garlic pieces or not, as you prefer.

"Of all the salads I serve when entertaining, this one is the most popular."

Antipasto Salad

5 ounces Italian salami, sliced to medium thickness
1 small red onion, thinly sliced
1 cup whole pitted ripe olives
1 14-ounce can artichoke hearts, drained and quartered
1 cup thinly sliced celery
1 cup cherry tomatoes, cut in half
½ cup sliced green bell pepper
8 ounces mozzarella cheese, cut into medium cubes
6 ounces shell or spiral pasta, cooked and drained
¾ cup Italian Dressing (see recipe, page 21)
½ pound mushrooms, sliced to medium thickness

1 Combine all ingredients except mushrooms; mix well. *Salad may be held for up to 3 hours at this point.*

2 Just before serving, add mushrooms and toss again.

*"...an Italian version of deviled eggs ...
easy and elegant."*

Stuffed Egg Salad

6 servings

6 hard-cooked eggs, shelled and cut in half lengthwise
2 teaspoons Dijon-style mustard
Salt and pepper to taste
5½ teaspoons olive oil
1 teaspoon chopped capers, rinsed and drained before chopping, plus 1 teaspoon more for garnish
3 anchovy fillets
2 medium tomatoes, cut into 6 thick slices, sprinkled with 1 tablespoon Italian Dressing (see recipe, page 21)
Red-leaf lettuce

1 Carefully remove yolks from whites and mash yolks with mustard, salt and pepper, olive oil and capers.

2 Refill egg whites with the mixture, topping each with half of an anchovy fillet and a few capers. Place each tomato slice on a lettuce leaf, then top tomato with 2 egg halves.

Instead of using Italian Dressing, you can sprinkle the tomato slices with olive oil, wine vinegar and salt and pepper to taste.

"I like to use two different greens in this traditional salad."

Arugula and Radicchio Salad with Olives

6 servings

8 ounces Italian oil-cured olives with pits
Italian Dressing
1 head radicchio
1 medium-size bunch arugula
1 head romaine lettuce, thinly sliced
16 cherry tomatoes
1 celery heart, finely chopped

Italian Dressing

Makes ¾ cup

¼ cup drained capers
1 garlic clove, pressed
1 shallot, minced
½ cup olive oil
½ teaspoon pepper
1 small dried red chili, sliced
½ teaspoon crushed fennel seed
1 tablespoon white Chianti *or* dry white wine
2 tablespoons lemon juice

1 Drain olives and pound until broken (with pits showing), but do not remove pits.

2 Pour Italian Dressing and olives into a salad bowl.

3 Place salad greens, tomatoes, and celery heart on top. Toss just before serving.

1 Combine all ingredients in a jar with tight-fitting lid and shake well.

*" This reminds me of my grandmother's
kitchen. It's her soup, which I've adapted
for quickness."*

Garbanzo and Pasta Soup

6 servings

2 tablespoons olive oil
1 garlic clove, minced
10 cups chicken stock
½ cup canned Italian plum tomatoes
¼ teaspoon dried rosemary *or* 1 teaspoon chopped fresh
2 15-ounce cans garbanzo beans (chick-peas)
Salt and pepper to taste
3 ounces small pasta, such as ditalini or avemaria
1 tablespoon chopped fresh parsley (preferably Italian flat leaf)

1 In large saucepan, heat olive oil, add garlic and sauté for 1 minute.

2 Add stock, tomatoes, rosemary, garbanzo beans and salt and pepper. Cover and simmer for 45 minutes.

3 Remove about half of garbanzo beans from broth, then press through food mill or puree in processor with rapid on-and-off turns. Return bean puree to broth.

4 Add pasta and continue cooking 15 minutes.

5 Stir in parsley. Adjust seasonings to taste and serve immediately.

"...very quick and satisfying."

Meatball Soup

4 to 6 servings

½ **pound ground beef**
1 **slice bread, soaked in milk
and squeezed dry**
½ **medium onion, finely
chopped**
1 **garlic clove, minced**
2 **tablespoons grated Romano
or Parmesan cheese (*or* a
combination of both), plus
more for garnish
Salt and pepper to taste**
2 **tablespoons tomato sauce**
1½ **teaspoons dry red wine**
1 **egg, beaten**
8 **cups beef stock**
½ **cup uncooked rice**
1 **teaspoon chopped fresh
parsley**

1 In a large bowl, thoroughly mix all ingredients except stock, rice and parsley, using your hands. Shape into ½-inch balls.

2 Bring stock to boil; drop meatballs in and add rice. (*Do not cover.*)

3 Lower heat so stock simmers; cook 15 minutes. Add parsley. Serve additional grated cheese separately for sprinkling over soup.

"I've been making this as long as I can remember. My family loves it."

Minestrone

8 to 10 servings

¼ cup olive oil
1 garlic clove, minced
1 medium onion, thinly sliced, then cut in half
2 celery stalks, sliced
2 cups shredded cabbage
2 cups sliced carrots
1 16-ounce can cannellini beans, rinsed and drained
1 28-ounce can Italian plum tomatoes, crushed by hand (including liquid)
1 10-ounce package frozen chopped spinach (unthawed)
½ teaspoon dried basil
1 tablespoon minced fresh parsley
¼ teaspoon dried sage
Salt and pepper to taste
½ cup uncooked rice (optional)
¼ cup ditalini *or* other small, hollow pasta (optional)
8 cups beef stock
¼ cup grated Parmesan cheese

1 Heat oil in a stockpot, add garlic, onion, celery, cabbage and carrot and sauté 10 minutes, stirring occasionally.

2 Add all other ingredients except Parmesan cheese; cover and simmer 45 minutes.

3 Add Parmesan cheese and stir well; simmer another 5 minutes and serve.

*"I make this sensational cold soup the day
ahead. It's great to have ready after a
hectic day."*

Cold Zucchini and Leek Soup

6 to 8 servings

2 tablespoons olive oil
1 tablespoon butter
2 leeks, white part only, cut into ½-inch slices
1 medium onion, thinly sliced
4 scallions, both white and green parts, cut into ½-inch slices
2 garlic cloves, minced
5 zucchini, unpeeled, cut into ½-inch slices
4 small white potatoes, peeled and cut into ¼-inch slices (approximately 2 cups)
4 to 5 cups chicken stock
1 tablespoon lemon juice
½ teaspoon salt
¼ teaspoon pepper
1 teaspoon *each* of marjoram, thyme, rosemary and savory
2 teaspoons Worcestershire sauce
1 cup whipping cream, or more as needed
2 tablespoons chopped chives (garnish)

1 Heat olive oil and butter in 4- to 5-quart saucepan and sauté leeks, onion, scallions, garlic, zucchini and potatoes until slightly softened, 5 to 10 minutes, stirring frequently.

2 Add chicken stock and lemon juice and bring to boil. Add salt and pepper and herbs. Simmer until vegetables are soft, about 25 minutes.

3 Puree soup in blender or processor in several batches. Stir in Worcestershire sauce and cream. (If soup is too thick, add more cream.) Allow to cool, then refrigerate.

4 Serve cold, garnished with chives.

" The spinach adds body to a great old standby."

Spinach Stracciatella Soup

6 servings

6 cups beef *or* chicken stock
1 pound fresh spinach, leaves only, cooked, drained and very finely chopped
3 eggs, beaten
2 tablespoons grated Parmesan *or* Romano cheese (*or* a combination of both)
¼ teaspoon salt
¼ teaspoon pepper
   Pinch of nutmeg
1 lemon, thinly sliced (garnish)

1 Bring stock to boil in a 3-quart saucepan.

2 Stir in spinach and cook 1 minute.

3 Lightly beat eggs, cheese and seasonings.

4 Pour egg mixture into stock, whisking constantly as threads form. *(The egg mixture is intended to curdle.)* Simmer 1 minute.

5 Remove from heat and season to taste. Garnish with lemon and serve at once.

"One of the first things my mother taught me to make was this basic sauce. The Bolognese is the version with meat."

Pomodoro Sauce

Makes about 8 cups,
enough for 2 pounds pasta

2 medium onions, coarsely
  chopped
¼ cup olive oil
1 garlic clove, minced
1 carrot, grated
2 28-ounce cans crushed
  Italian plum tomatoes
½ cup water *or* beef stock
½ teaspoon dried thyme
½ teaspoon dried basil
½ teaspoon salt
1 teaspoon sugar
  Pepper to taste

1 In large saucepan, sauté onions with oil until almost soft. Add garlic and sauté 1 minute.

2 Add all other ingredients, bring to boiling point and simmer uncovered over low heat for 1 hour.

Bolognese Sauce

Makes about 5 cups

3 cups Pomodoro Sauce (see
  recipe above)
1 pound lean ground beef
1 sweet *or* hot Italian sausage,
  casing removed (optional)
½ teaspoon salt
¼ teaspoon pepper

1 Heat Pomodoro Sauce in large saucepan. Meanwhile, crumble beef and sausage into medium skillet and sauté briefly over medium-high heat to render excess fat. Drain meat and add to sauce. Season with salt and pepper.

2 Simmer uncovered 30 minutes to 1 hour. Adjust seasonings to taste.

". . . my updated version of Fettuccine Alfredo."

Linguine with Gorgonzola Sauce

6 to 8 servings

3 tablespoons butter
1 cup whipping cream
½ pound Gorgonzola cheese, crumbled
⅓ cup grated Parmesan cheese
1 pound linguine, cooked and drained
1 tablespoon chopped fresh parsley (garnish)

1 Melt butter in large saucepan over low heat.

2 Add cream and heat gently.

3 Add Gorgonzola cheese; stir until smooth.

4 Add Parmesan cheese and linguine. Toss gently and thoroughly until well heated.

5 Sprinkle with parsley and serve at once.

"I have to give my Aunt Cecilia credit for this. I simply altered the method."

Linguine with Seafood and Herb Sauce

6 to 8 servings

1 pound linguine *or* spaghetti
⅓ cup combination of olive oil and vegetable oil, proportioned to taste.
½ cup (1 stick) butter
3 to 4 garlic cloves, minced
2 pounds uncooked shelled medium shrimp *or* combination of shrimp and crabmeat
⅓ cup lemon juice
3 tablespoons *each*, chopped fresh herbs *or* 1 tablespoon each dried: basil, parsley and oregano
½ teaspoon salt
    Pepper to taste
3 tablespoons grated Parmesan cheese

1 Cook pasta until al dente; drain and rinse with boiling water. Set aside.

2 Heat oil and butter in large skillet or ovenproof serving dish. Sauté garlic and shrimp until shrimp just turn pink. Add crabmeat if desired.

3 Add lemon juice and herbs; simmer 5 minutes. Season to taste.

4 Add pasta, toss gently to blend, and heat. Sprinkle with Parmesan.

" . . . simple but impressive for company."

Pasta with Smoked Salmon and Golden Caviar

6 servings

1½ **pounds thin spaghetti**
¾ **cup (1½ sticks) butter, plus up to 4 tablespoons (½ stick) more for pasta**
2 **cups whipping cream**
½ **pound smoked salmon, thinly sliced and cut into ½-inch pieces**
White pepper to taste
1 **4-ounce can golden caviar (about 1 tablespoon per serving), room temperature**

1 Cook pasta until al dente; rinse and drain. Blend up to 4 tablespoons butter into pasta to moisten.

2 Melt ¾ cup butter in heavy large skillet. Add cream and bring to a boil, stirring occasionally. Reduce heat to medium and cook sauce until reduced, about 5 minutes.

3 Add smoked salmon and white pepper. (The smoked salmon will probably eliminate the need for salt.)

4 Add pasta to sauce and toss gently but thoroughly. Heat to warm if necessary.

5 Serve immediately with a spoonful of caviar on top or on the side of each serving.

"Even my mother loves this untraditional pasta dish."

Pasta with Broccoli and Goat Cheese

4 to 6 servings

1¼ **cups whipping cream**
¼ **cup milk**
¼ **teaspoon minced garlic**
6 **ounces Bucheron goat cheese, rind removed,** *or* **Montrachet goat cheese, cut into 1-inch cubes**
1 **teaspoon white wine vinegar**
Coarse salt and pepper to taste
1 **pound angel-hair pasta** *or* **thin spaghetti**
1 **cup small broccoli florets, steamed or stir-fried crisp-tender**
1½ **tablespoons chopped fresh basil leaves**
1½ **tablespoons chopped fresh parsley (preferably Italian flat leaf)**
1 **teaspoon chopped fresh rosemary** *or* ½ **teaspoon dried**

1 Heat cream, milk and garlic in heavy medium saucepan over low heat until bubbles form around edges. Remove from heat and whisk in cheese until smooth.

2 Add wine vinegar and salt and pepper. Remove from heat and let stand 15 minutes.

3 Cook pasta until al dente.

4 While pasta is cooking, add broccoli florets to sauce and return to low heat to warm. Stir herbs into warmed sauce.

5 Drain pasta and add to sauce. Toss mixture gently but thoroughly. Adjust seasonings to taste. Serve immediately.

"...a real classic. I use Pomodoro Sauce as the base."

Tagliarini Arrabiati

4 to 6 servings

¼ **cup butter, plus 3 tablespoons more for pasta**
3 **tablespoons minced chives**
¾ **to 1 teaspoon dried red pepper flakes or to taste**
2 **tablespoons dry white wine**
3 **cups Pomodoro Sauce (see recipe, page 33)**
6 **whole Italian plum tomatoes, peeled, seeded, drained and crushed *or* one 14½-ounce can peeled whole Italian plum tomatoes, seeded, drained and crushed**
1 **pound tagliarini, fettuccine *or* other flat pasta**
   Salt and pepper to taste
   Grated Parmesan cheese

1 Melt ¼ cup butter in medium saucepan and lightly sauté chives.

2 Add red pepper flakes and wine and blend thoroughly.

3 Add Pomodoro Sauce and tomatoes. Simmer uncovered 45 minutes.

4 Meanwhile, cook tagliarini until al dente; drain. Toss with remaining tablespoons butter. Keep warm.

5 For sauce, adjust seasonings to taste. Continue cooking 10 minutes, then pour over tagliarini.

6 Serve with Parmesan cheese.

"No matter how busy I am, I just can't deprive my family of pizza. This quick crust recipe is my solution."

Pizza Crust Rapido

Makes enough for one 12-inch pizza

¾ cup self-rising flour
¾ cup all purpose flour
½ teaspoon salt
½ cup plus 1 tablespoon lukewarm water (90°F to 105°F)
1 tablespoon olive oil, plus 2 more tablespoons for painting crust

1 Preheat oven to 425°F. Thoroughly mix flours and salt. (Use processor if possible.) Mix water and 1 tablespoon olive oil, either by hand or by pouring into processor while motor is running.

2 Remove dough and knead by hand until smooth, 2 to 3 minutes. Let dough rest 5 to 10 minutes before rolling out and placing in pizza pan or on baking sheet in a 12-inch circle. Paint with olive oil.

3 Bake 10 minutes. Apply toppings to pizza immediately and bake 5 to 10 minutes.

Pizza Margherita

Makes one 12-inch pizza

1 12-inch pizza crust, prebaked
4 teaspoons olive oil
2 heaping cups grated mozzarella cheese
2 large tomatoes or 6 Italian plum tomatoes, sliced
¼ cup chopped fresh basil *or* 1 heaping tablespoon dried

1 Preheat oven to 425°F. Brush prebaked pizza crust with olive oil and sprinkle with all but ¼ cup of the mozzarella.

2 Place tomato slices over cheese; sprinkle remaining mozzarella on top. Sprinkle basil over topping and bake pizza until nicely browned.

"This is gone before I can turn around. I usually make four when I'm entertaining."

Pesto Cocktail Pizza

Makes two 12-inch pizzas

½ cup olive oil
2 cups tightly packed fresh basil leaves
¼ cup tightly packed fresh parsley
¾ cup grated Parmesan cheese
2 garlic cloves, cut in half
½ teaspoon salt
Pepper to taste
2 tablespoons pine nuts
2 12-inch pizza crusts (see recipe, page 45)

1 Preheat oven to 425°F. For pesto sauce, place oil, basil, parsley, ½ cup cheese, garlic, salt and pepper and pine nuts in processor or blender.

2 Using on-and-off turns, process or blend ingredients for about 2 minutes, scraping down sides of blender or processor bowl once or twice.

3 Spread half of pesto sauce evenly over each pizza, coming to within ½ inch of edge.

4 Bake until topping bubbles, 4 to 5 minutes.

5 Sprinkle with remaining ¼ cup cheese. Slice and serve immediately.

"My daughter helps me make this, as I used to help my mother. Ours is quicker than hers, but just as good."

Sausage and Sage Pizza

Makes one 12-inch pizza

3 sweet *or* hot Italian sausages
  (*or* a combination of both),
  casings removed
1 heaping cup grated
  mozzarella cheese
1 12-inch pizza crust (see
  recipe, p. 45)
5 tablespoons grated Romano
  cheese
1 heaping tablespoon chopped
  fresh sage *or* 1 teaspoon dried
  Juice of ½ lemon

1 Preheat oven to 425°F. Crumble sausage meat into small pieces. Either cook in microwave briefly or sauté (3 to 5 minutes) to draw out excess fat; drain on paper towels.

2 Sprinkle mozzarella evenly over pizza crust, then distribute sausage meat evenly over crust.

3 Sprinkle Romano cheese, then sage, evenly over meat.

4 Bake pizza with topping until nicely browned, about 10 minutes.

5 Before serving, squeeze lemon juice over top of pizza.

"...easy, fast, and delizioso!"

Mussels Oregano

6 to 8 servings

36 mussels, scrubbed and debearded
½ cup (1 stick) butter, melted
4 small garlic cloves, minced
½ cup seasoned breadcrumbs
2 teaspoons dried oregano, crumbled
2 tablespoons chopped fresh parsley, plus 2 tablespoons more for garnish
1 small onion, minced
¼ cup dry white wine
½ teaspoon salt
¼ teaspoon pepper

1 In 4- to 5-quart saucepan, heat 2 inches water to a boil. Add mussels, cover and steam until shells open. Remove and open mussels, discarding top shells. Loosen each mussel from shell, but put it back in bottom shell. Reserve cooking juices.

2 Preheat oven to 375°F. Combine all remaining ingredients except parsley for garnish, using enough reserved cooking juice to make a loose paste.

3 Put crumb mixture on top of each mussel and place the shells on a baking sheet. Bake 10 minutes and then broil to brown, about 3 minutes. Sprinkle with parsley and serve at once.

"... a guaranteed success."

Scampi

6 tablespoons (¾ stick) butter
2 pounds uncooked jumbo shrimp, shelled and deveined, tails left on
1 teaspoon dried rosemary
1 teaspoon dried oregano
6 small garlic cloves, cut into fourths
¼ cup dry white wine *or* dry vermouth
4 teaspoons grated lemon peel
2 tablespoons lemon juice
2 tablespoons chopped fresh parsley
¼ teaspoon salt
Pepper to taste

1 Melt butter in large skillet. While butter is melting, prepare shrimp by sprinkling with rosemary and oregano.

2 Sauté garlic chunks in butter until golden. Remove with slotted spoon and discard. Add shrimp and cook, stirring, until shrimp turn pink, about 3 minutes (depending on size).

3 Sprinkle wine, lemon peel and juice and parsley over shrimp. Stir and turn shrimp over medium-high heat 5 minutes longer. Season with salt and pepper before serving.

" . . . light and tangy . . . a perfect warm-weather dish."

Baked Halibut Limone

6 servings

3 **pounds halibut, cut into 6**
  serving pieces ¾ inch thick
  Salt and pepper to taste
1 **teaspoon paprika**
2 **garlic cloves, minced**
¼ **cup minced fresh parsley**
½ **cup seasoned breadcrumbs**
2 **lemons, sliced, plus 2 more**
  thinly sliced lemons for
  garnish
1 **tablespoon butter**

1 Preheat oven to 375°F. Sprinkle both sides of fish with salt and pepper and paprika.

2 Place fish in a buttered shallow baking dish and sprinkle with garlic, parsley and breadcrumbs.

3 Place lemon slices on fish and add water almost to top of fish.

4 Bake uncovered 20 to 30 minutes, until fish is firm and crumbs are golden brown.

5 Remove lemon slices, dot with butter and place under broiler briefly until browned. Garnish with thin lemon slices.

"The herb stuffing enhances the delicate flavor of the sole."

Stuffed Fillet of Sole with Watercress Sauce

4 to 6 servings

6 fennel sprigs
4 parsley sprigs
5 small scallions
2 small garlic cloves, chopped
4 ounces cream cheese
1½ slices bread, crumbled
6 medium mushrooms, coarsely chopped
8 to 10 sole fillets (about 1 pound), sprinkled with salt and pepper to taste and juice of 1 lemon
5 tablespoons butter, melted
⅓ cup breadcrumbs

1 Preheat oven to 300°F. In processor, finely puree first four ingredients. Add cream cheese and bread; mix well. Remove from processor and stir in mushrooms.

2 Place fish "skin" side down. Place spoonful of stuffing on each fillet. Roll up, starting with small ends. Place seam side down in buttered shallow baking dish. Combine breadcrumbs and melted butter and spread on top. Cover tightly with foil.

3 Bake 15 minutes. Uncover and bake until fish flakes, about 10 minutes.

Watercress Sauce

Makes ½ cup

¼ cup watercress leaves
2 scallions
3 egg yolks
⅓ cup hot fish stock or clam juice
⅓ cup whipping cream, warmed
Salt and pepper to taste
6 sprigs watercress (garnish)

1 In processor or blender, process watercress leaves, scallions and yolks until smooth. With motor on slowly add fish stock in a stream, then add cream, blending until smooth.

2 Transfer to small saucepan and cook, stirring constantly, over low heat until slightly thickened, 1 to 2 minutes. Season to taste with salt and pepper. Spoon over fillets and garnish with watercress sprigs.

*"'Fantastico!' was Uncle Carlo's response to
this impressive dish."*

Seafood Baked in a Package

6 to 8 servings

3 pounds swordfish *or* halibut, cut into serving pieces ½ inch thick
Salt and pepper
⅓ cup (⅔ stick) butter, room temperature
1½ teaspoons garlic puree
1 tablespoon lemon juice
1 teaspoon dried tarragon
¾ pound uncooked small or medium shrimp, shelled and deveined
¼ cup dry white wine
¼ cup whipping cream
2 tablespoons chopped fresh parsley (garnish)

1 Preheat oven to 350°F. Sprinkle fish with salt and pepper. Mix butter, garlic, lemon juice and tarragon until well blended. Using half of butter mixture, coat one side of fish and place buttered side down on half a sheet of heavy-duty aluminum foil that measures 48 inches in length.

2 Place shrimp on top of fish and dot with remaining butter mixture. Pour wine over. Fold other half of sheet over fish; seal and crimp foil.

3 Bake 25 to 35 minutes in upper part of oven.

4 Remove fish and shrimp and keep warm on a heated serving platter loosely covered with aluminum foil.

5 Pour off juices into small skillet. Add cream and reduce to ¾ to 1 cup. Pour over fish, sprinkle with parsley and serve at once.

"Everyone ends up in the kitchen when I'm cooking this fragrant dish."

Chicken Marengo

6 servings

6 serving pieces frying chicken
(legs with thighs attached
and breast halves)
1 teaspoon salt
½ teaspoon pepper
½ teaspoon garlic salt
2 tablespoons olive oil
2 tablespoons (¼ stick) butter
1 large onion, coarsely chopped
2 small garlic cloves, minced
¼ pound mushrooms, sliced
½ cup dry Marsala
1 cup chicken stock
¾ teaspoon dried oregano
1 3½-ounce can pitted black
olives, cut in half crosswise
3 tablespoons instant flour
(optional)
1 tablespoon chopped fresh
parsley (garnish)

1 Season chicken with salt and pepper and garlic salt.

2 Heat oil and butter in large skillet and brown chicken on all sides. Remove chicken.

3 In same skillet, sauté onion, garlic and mushrooms for 5 minutes. Remove with slotted spoon, set aside and keep warm. Pour off excess oil and wipe out skillet.

4 Return chicken to skillet and add wine, stock, oregano and olives. Cover and simmer until chicken is tender, about 35 minutes. Add sautéed mushrooms, garlic and onions. (If thicker sauce is desired, combine instant flour with 3 tablespoons cooking liquid and add to skillet for last 10 minutes of cooking, leaving skillet uncovered.) Sprinkle with parsley before serving.

" . . . a much more economical version than the one made with veal, and great for picnics."

Chicken Tonnato d'Este

6 servings

4¼ cups chicken stock
6 chicken breast halves, skinned
½ cup mayonnaise
¼ cup dry white wine
4 flat anchovy fillets
1 tablespoon oil from anchovies
1 7-ounce can water-packed tuna, drained
2 tablespoons lemon juice
¼ teaspoon dried oregano
Salt and pepper to taste
1 tablespoon capers, drained (garnish)
2 tablespoons chopped fresh parsley (garnish)
1 lemon, sliced (garnish)

1 Bring 4 cups chicken stock to boil in covered saucepan. Poach chicken breasts 15 minutes and allow to cool in stock.

2 For tonnato sauce, in blender or processor, combine mayonnaise, wine, ¼ cup stock, anchovies and oil from anchovies, tuna, lemon juice and oregano and process until well blended. Season to taste with salt and pepper.

3 Remove bones from chicken breasts and cut meat into ½-inch-thick slices. Layer on serving platter, so that they overlap slightly. Pour tonnato sauce over all. Sprinkle capers and parsley on top and garnish with lemon slices. Serve cold or at room temperature.

*"I know this looks complicated, but it's
actually very easy and very good."*

Chicken Saltimbocca

6 servings

6 **chicken breast halves, skinned and boned**
6 **thin slices prosciutto (2 by 4 inches)**
6 **thin slices provolone cheese (2 by 4 inches)**
½ **teaspoon salt**
⅛ **teaspoon pepper**
1 **teaspoon paprika**
½ **cup all purpose flour**
1 **cup breadcrumbs**
1 **teaspoon dried tarragon**
3 **eggs, beaten**
3 **tablespoons butter**
½ **cup dry white wine *or* dry Marsala**

1 Place each breast half between 2 pieces of waxed paper and pound to ⅛-inch thickness with flat side of large knife. Use rolling pin also, if necessary.

2 Lay piece of prosciutto and piece of cheese on each breast half. Roll up jelly roll fashion, tucking in ends. Fasten with wooden toothpicks.

3 Combine salt and pepper and paprika with flour. In separate dish, combine breadcrumbs with tarragon. Roll chicken in flour, then in eggs and in crumb mixture. Chill 30 minutes (chicken can be placed in freezer 15 minutes).

4 Preheat oven to 350°F. Heat butter in large skillet and sauté chicken rolls until well browned on all sides. Remove toothpicks.

5 Place chicken rolls in baking dish and bake for 10 minutes.

6 Add wine to skillet and heat, scraping up any browned bits. Pour over chicken rolls and serve at once.

"This is another old family recipe. I don't know exactly which of my ancestors the 'madre' in the name refers to."

Chicken Cacciatore Madre

6 servings

¼ cup olive oil
6 serving pieces frying chicken (legs with thighs attached and breast halves)
1¼ cups all purpose flour, seasoned with 1 teaspoon paprika and salt and pepper to taste
½ cup thinly sliced onion
2 medium garlic cloves, minced
⅔ cup dry Marsala
1 green bell pepper, cut into julienne strips
2 carrots, thinly sliced
1 celery stalk, thinly sliced
1 cup canned crushed Italian plum tomatoes
1 teaspoon dried basil
1 teaspoon dried thyme
1 teaspoon dried oregano
Salt and pepper to taste

1 Heat oil in heavy large skillet.

2 Coat chicken with seasoned flour, shaking off excess.

3 Brown chicken on all sides over moderate heat, being careful not to crowd skillet. Remove and set aside.

4 In same skillet sauté onion and garlic 3 minutes.

5 Turn heat to high and add wine, scraping up browned bits from bottom of skillet.

6 Add chicken, vegetables and herbs. Cook 5 to 7 minutes.

7 Cover and simmer until tender, about 30 minutes. Add herbs. Adjust seasoning to taste.

"...my version of an unforgettable dish I had at a restaurant in Venice one late summer afternoon."

Chicken Oregano

6 servings

3 pounds chicken breast
halves, skinned and boned
2 tablespoons olive oil
2 tablespoons butter
⅓ cup all purpose flour
1 large egg beaten with 2
tablespoons water
Salt and pepper to taste
1 rounded teaspoon dried
oregano *or* 1 tablespoon
finely chopped fresh
1 pound provolone cheese,
thinly sliced

1 Place each breast half between 2 pieces of waxed paper and pound to ¼-inch thickness with flat side of large knife. Use rolling pin also, if necessary.

2 Heat oil and butter in large skillet.

3 Dip breasts in flour and shake off excess. Dip in egg mixture, allowing excess to drip off, and sauté in skillet a few pieces at a time. Turn once, browning on both sides, about 3 minutes altogether. Remove and drain as they are done. Meanwhile, preheat oven to 350°F.

4 Arrange chicken in buttered shallow baking dish. Sprinkle with salt and pepper and oregano. Top with cheese slices.

5 Cover with aluminum foil and bake 15 minutes. Remove foil and continue baking until nicely browned, 15 to 20 minutes.

"...an inventive, economical, and delicious dish."

Chicken in Cream and Herb Sauce

6 servings
Chicken breasts or veal may be substituted.

6 chicken thighs (1½ to 2 pounds), skinned and boned
All purpose flour seasoned with salt and pepper to taste (for dredging)
3 tablespoons butter
3 tablespoons olive oil
½ cup dry white wine
1 tablespoon lemon juice
½ cup whipping cream
½ teaspoon dried thyme
Salt and pepper to taste
2 tablespoons minced fresh parsley, plus 2 tablespoons more for garnish
1 lemon, sliced (garnish)
1 tablespoon capers, rinsed and drained (garnish)

1 Place chicken between sheets of plastic wrap, and with a heavy wooden mallet, pound evenly and gently until about ¼ inch thick. Dredge chicken with seasoned flour.

2 In large skillet, heat 1½ tablespoons *each* butter and oil. Add as many pieces of chicken as will fit without crowding. Cook quickly, just until meat loses pinkness when slashed, about 1½ minutes per side. Place on hot platter; keep warm.

3 Cook remaining pieces, adding more butter and oil as needed; add to platter and keep warm. (Chicken may be placed in 200°F oven while sauce is prepared.)

4 Add wine and lemon juice to skillet and simmer over moderately high heat, stirring to blend in browned particles. Boil, reducing to about half.

5 Add whipping cream, thyme and parsley; boil until sauce thickens slightly. Pour any meat juices from warming platter into sauce.

6 Adjust sauce for seasoning to taste. Pour over meat and garnish with parsley, lemon slices and capers.

*"The savory mustard sauce is a wonderful
counterpoint to the livers."*

Chicken Livers Senape

6 to 8 servings

¼ cup (½ stick) butter (or more)
1 medium onion, chopped medium fine
1 pound mushrooms, sliced to medium thickness
1½ pounds chicken livers, cleaned and separated (not cut) and patted dry
3 tablespoons dry white wine
¾ cup whipping cream
1½ tablespoons Dijon-style mustard
Salt and pepper to taste
Pinch of sugar
1 tablespoon minced fresh parsley

1 Melt butter in large skillet and sauté onion and mushrooms until soft. Remove with a slotted spoon and reserve.

2 Sauté livers in same skillet until lightly browned, adding more butter if necessary.

3 Add wine and heat to boiling. Stir in cream, mustard, salt and pepper, sugar and parsley. Blend well. Simmer until livers are no longer pink and sauce is thickened.

4 Return mushroom and onion mixture to livers just long enough to reheat. Serve at once.

". . . a great alternative to chicken or veal."

Turkey Breasts Marsala

6 servings

6 turkey breast fillets
¼ teaspoon dried basil
¼ teaspoon dried oregano
¼ cup all purpose flour
3 tablespoons butter
6 tablespoons dry Marsala
6 tablespoons chicken stock
¼ teaspoon salt
  Pinch of pepper
1 tablespoon chopped fresh
  parsley (garnish)

1 Lay each turkey slice between 2 pieces of waxed paper and pound thin with flat side of large knife. Dip into a mixture of basil, oregano and flour.

2 Heat butter to sizzling in large skillet. Sauté turkey breasts until golden brown, 2 to 3 minutes on each side.

3 Add Marsala, stock and salt and pepper. Cook uncovered about 3 minutes, turning once. Pour pan juices over, garnish with parsley and serve immediately.

"I've been teaching my husband how to prepare some of my dishes. He's quite proud of his lamb steaks."

Lamb Steaks with Vermouth and Rosemary

6 servings

6 **lamb steaks from the boned rib *or* loin, trimmed into round steaks 1 inch thick**
1 **garlic clove, minced**
1 **teaspoon salt**
¼ **teaspoon pepper**
½ **teaspoon chopped dried rosemary *or* 1 teaspoon finely chopped fresh**
3 **tablespoons butter**
1 **onion, chopped**
2 **tablespoons chopped shallot**
½ **teaspoon grated lemon peel**
½ **pound small mushrooms**
½ **cup dry vermouth**
3 **tablespoons minced fresh parsley (garnish)**

1 Preheat oven to 350°F. Rub lamb with a mixture of garlic, salt and pepper and rosemary.

2 Heat 2 tablespoons butter in a large skillet. Sauté meat slices over moderate heat until well browned on one side. Pour off any excess fat from pan. Turn and brown other side. Remove and keep warm in ovenproof serving dish.

3 Add remaining tablespoon butter to same skillet and heat. Add onion, shallot, lemon peel and mushrooms. Sauté until softened. Add vermouth and pour over meat.

4 Cover serving dish loosely with aluminum foil and bake about 10 minutes for pink lamb, 15 minutes for well done. Remove foil and bake 5 more minutes. Season to taste and sprinkle with chopped parsley before serving.

*"I still make this the same way as my
mother. It can't really be improved upon."*

Veal Scaloppine with Lemon

6 servings

1½ **pounds veal scaloppine from the top round, sliced about ¼ inch thick**
1 **cup all purpose flour**
2 **tablespoons olive oil**
½ **cup (1 stick) butter**
Juice of 1 lemon
3 **tablespoons finely chopped fresh parsley**
Salt and pepper to taste
2 **lemons, thinly sliced (garnish)**

1 Pound veal scallops between 2 sheets of waxed paper until they are about ⅛ inch thick. Blot meat with paper towels, then lightly dust with flour and shake off excess.

2 Heat 1 tablespoon oil and half the butter in large skillet over medium heat. When butter and oil are sizzling, brown veal slices, a few at a time, on both sides. Remove and keep warm. Add butter and oil between batches as needed.

3 Remove skillet from heat and add lemon juice and any remaining butter, scraping browned bits from bottom of pan.

4 Add parsley and veal and season to taste. Cook over medium heat about 5 minutes.

5 Remove veal to platter, pouring juices over all and garnishing with lemon slices.

*"I use avocado to add a California touch
to this dish."*

Veal Scaloppine with Avocado

6 to 8 servings

2 pounds veal scaloppine from the top round, sliced about ¼ inch thick)
1 teaspoon salt
½ teaspoon pepper
¼ cup all purpose flour
1 teaspoon dried oregano
8 tablespoons (1 stick) butter
2 tablespoons olive oil
½ cup dry vermouth
¾ cup chicken stock
4 tablespoons lemon juice
⅓ cup chopped fresh parsley
1 avocado, peeled and cut into 8 even slices

1 Pound meat between waxed paper until ⅛ inch thick. Combine next four ingredients. Coat veal in mixture; shake off excess and set aside.

2 Preheat oven to 300°F. In a large skillet, heat 5 tablespoons butter and the oil over moderately high heat. Sauté half of veal at a time until lightly browned, 2 to 3 minutes on each side. Remove to warm platter.

3 Add vermouth to skillet and boil, scraping up browned bits, until liquid is reduced by half. Add stock and 3 tablespoons lemon juice, stirring well. Add parsley. Remove from heat.

4 Sprinkle avocado with 1 tablespoon lemon juice. Bake in small ovenproof dish 5 minutes.

5 Meanwhile, boil sauce in skillet until slightly reduced, about 2 minutes. Lower heat and whisk in remaining butter, a teaspoonful at a time, until sauce is slightly thickened.

6 Place veal scallops on warm platter and surround with avocado slices. Pour sauce over and serve at once.

"Veal has been the source of inspiration for many great dishes in my family. This is one of my favorites."

Veal Chops with Anchovy and Caper Sauce

6 servings

½ cup vegetable oil
6 veal loin chops, ¾ inch thick
½ cup all purpose flour
6 tablespoons (¾ stick) butter
2 ounces boiled ham, finely minced
4 flat anchovy fillets
2 tablespoons capers, rinsed and drained
¼ cup brandy
6 tablespoons whipping cream
2 tablespoons chopped fresh parsley (garnish)

1 Heat oil in a heavy skillet large enough to accommodate chops.

2 Pat chops dry and coat with flour, shaking off excess. Sauté chops in very hot oil, turning once.

3 Meanwhile, melt butter in a small skillet and sauté ham over medium heat 1 minute. Add anchovies and capers, mashing ingredients down with fork to make a paste.

4 When chops are done, about 8 to 10 minutes, remove to heated oven-proof platter and keep warm in a 200°F oven with a piece of aluminum foil placed loosely over top.

5 Pour off excess oil from skillet in which chops were cooked. Add brandy, scraping up browned bits. Boil to reduce liquid by half, then pour into ham and anchovy mixture. Add cream, heating and stirring while it blends.

6 Pour sauce over chops and garnish with parsley.

*"Steak lovers, like my husband, find this
irresistible."*

Beef Tenderloin with Marsala

6 servings

3 teaspoons butter, plus 3
  tablespoons butter, melted
2 ounces thinly sliced pancetta
  (Italian dry-cured unsmoked
  bacon) *or* bacon
1 onion, thinly sliced
6 1-inch slices (about 2¼
  pounds) filet mignon
  Salt and pepper to taste
¾ cup dry Marsala
½ cup beef stock

1 Heat 3 teaspoons butter and pancetta or bacon in a skillet large enough to hold meat in one layer. Sauté until golden brown. Add onion and sauté until golden. Remove pancetta or bacon and onion with slotted spoon. Reserve bacon and discard onion.

2 Put beef slices in same skillet and pan-broil until quite brown, about 3 minutes on each side.

3 Season to taste with salt and pepper. Add melted butter, wine and stock and lower heat. Cook 2 more minutes on each side, turning once to coat slices with sauce. Remove meat, place on top of reserved bacon on serving platter, and keep warm. Boil sauce until slightly reduced, 2 to 3 minutes. Pour over meat and serve.

*"I make this especially for my Uncle Carlo.
It's his favorite old-country dish."*

Gnocchi

6 servings

4 cups milk
2 cups semolina
½ cup (1 stick) butter, room
temperature
1 cup grated Parmesan cheese
1 cup grated Romano cheese
4 eggs, beaten
Pomodoro Sauce (optional,
see recipe, page 33)

1 Preheat oven to 400°F. Bring milk to boil in 4-quart saucepan. While milk is boiling, pour in semolina very slowly, stirring constantly with a wooden spoon to prevent lumps. Cook and stir 3 to 4 minutes.

2 Remove saucepan from heat and stir in butter.

3 Mix Parmesan and Romano cheeses together. Mix half of cheese with beaten eggs and stir into semolina. Spread in buttered 8½ × 13-inch baking dish and sprinkle remaining cheese over top.

4 Bake until golden brown, about 15 minutes. Cut into squares or diamond shapes and serve. Accompany with Pomodoro Sauce if desired.

"...an unusual and delicious vegetable dish."

Peas with Prosciutto and Pine Nuts

6 servings

6 **slices prosciutto, trimmed and cut into julienne strips (reserve some fat)**
⅓ **cup pine nuts, toasted (toast 10 minutes at 350°F)**
1½ **cups chicken stock**
4 **lettuce leaves, shredded**
1¼ **packages (15 ounces) frozen peas**
  Salt and pepper to taste

1 Sauté prosciutto in several pieces of its own fat over low heat for about 2 minutes. Add pine nuts and continue cooking for about 1 minute. Remove from heat and set aside.

2 Bring stock to boil in medium saucepan. Add lettuce and peas and return to boil. Remove from heat; strain.

3 Pour vegetables into medium serving bowl. Add pine nut–prosciutto mixture and season to taste. Serve immediately.

*"This is for my guests who are always
trying to figure out how I make this dish."*

Carrots Marsala

3 tablespoons butter
14 medium carrots, cut into ⅛-inch diagonal slices
¾ cup good-quality dry Marsala
1 tablespoon chicken stock *or* water (optional)
2 tablespoons chopped fresh parsley

1 Heat butter in large skillet with tight-fitting lid. Sauté carrot slices until carrots are well coated with butter, 2 to 3 minutes.

2 Add Marsala and cover. Cook over medium to low heat until carrots are tender and liquid is reduced, 8 to 10 minutes. (If liquid reduces before carrots are tender, add 1 tablespoon chicken stock or water.)

3 Sprinkle with parsley before serving.

"...a quick alternative to eggplant Parmesan."

Stuffed Eggplant Suocera

6 servings

3 small eggplants, unpeeled
¾ pound mushrooms, sliced to medium thickness
¼ cup minced onion
3 small garlic cloves, minced
3 tablespoons minced fresh parsley
3 large tomatoes, seeded, drained and chopped
1 teaspoon dried oregano
2 teaspoons dried basil
1 teaspoon dried thyme
Salt and pepper to taste
3 tablespoons olive oil
¼ cup grated Romano cheese
Parsley sprigs (garnish)

1 Preheat oven to 375°F. Bake eggplants 30 minutes. (Do not turn off oven.)

2 Run under cold water to cool, then scoop and cut out center of each, leaving a very thin shell. Chop centers and mix with all other ingredients except oil, Romano cheese and parsley.

3 Heat oil in large skillet and sauté mixture for 5 minutes.

4 With a slotted spoon, fill eggplant shells with mixture and top with Romano cheese. Bake 10 minutes.

5 Place under broiler to brown cheese lightly, about 2 minutes.

6 Garnish each serving with sprig of parsley.

While shells will hold the filling for an attractive presentation, they may not be tender enough to eat.

"These are as hard to resist as potato chips."

Fried Zucchini

6 servings

1 **pound zucchini, cut into ⅛-inch slices**
1 **teaspoon salt**
⅔ **cup sifted all purpose flour, or more**
1 **cup water**
Vegetable oil (for frying)

1 Sprinkle zucchini slices with salt; allow to stand 30 minutes. Drain and pat dry.

2 Gradually add flour to water, beating in with fork, until batter has consistency of sour cream. Add more flour if necessary.

3 Add enough oil to large skillet to come ¾ inch up side. Heat to 375°F.

4 Dip zucchini slices in batter and drop them into oil. *Do not crowd skillet.*

5 Fry until bottoms have golden crusts, then turn slices over. Drain, salt if necessary and serve at once.

"... a hearty, very Italian side dish."

Cannellini Beans with Italian Sausage

6 servings

1 tablespoon olive oil
3 hot Italian sausages
3 sweet Italian sausages
4 garlic cloves, minced
1 tablespoon chopped fresh sage
   or 1 rounded teaspoon dried
1 28-ounce can Italian plum
   tomatoes, drained and
   coarsely chopped
2 16-ounce cans cannellini
   beans, rinsed and drained
   Salt and pepper to taste

1 Heat oil in an ovenproof, flameproof medium casserole and sauté sausages 15 minutes. Drain off excess fat.

2 Add garlic and sage and sauté until garlic is golden. Cool and slice sausages into 1½-inch pieces.

3 Add tomatoes and beans and simmer until well cooked, about 15 minutes, stirring occasionally. Season to taste.

This may be held in the oven for 30 minutes at 300°F.

"A visit to my grandmother in Milan inspired this dish."

Artichokes Milanese

6 to 8 servings

⅓ cup butter
1 cup sliced mushrooms
1 tablespoon fine seasoned breadcrumbs
¼ teaspoon garlic puree
2 tablespoons lemon juice
2 9-ounce packages frozen artichoke hearts, thawed and drained
½ cup grated Parmesan cheese

1 Preheat oven to 350°F. Heat butter and sauté mushrooms in medium skillet until crisp-tender.

2 Mix together breadcrumbs, garlic puree and lemon juice. Stir mixture into mushrooms.

3 Arrange artichoke hearts in a buttered shallow ovenproof serving dish. Spoon mushroom mixture over artichokes and sprinkle cheese over all.

4 Bake 25 to 30 minutes.

Tomatoes Stuffed with Basil Zucchini

6 servings

6 medium tomatoes, tops sliced off and pulp scooped out
Salt and pepper to taste
¼ cup olive oil
6 medium zucchini, unpeeled, thinly sliced
1 tablespoon chopped fresh basil leaves *or* 1½ teaspoons dried
3 tablespoons butter
2 tablespoons chopped garlic
2 tablespoons chopped fresh parsley
1 tablespoon chopped fresh parsley (garnish)

1 Preheat oven to 375°F. Lightly sprinkle insides of tomatoes with salt and pepper and drain upside down on paper towels.

2 Heat olive oil in large skillet. Stir-fry zucchini and basil over medium-high heat for 8 minutes. Remove and drain on paper towels. Season with salt and pepper.

3 Heat butter in very small skillet and sauté garlic and 2 tablespoons parsley 2 minutes. Divide mixture among tomatoes, spooning some in bottom of each.

4 Fill tomatoes with zucchini and garnish with parsley. Place in a buttered shallow baking dish and bake uncovered 15 minutes.

"... a colorful dish with several interesting textures."

Green Beans with Mortadella

6 servings

5 teaspoons salt
1½ pounds fresh green beans, ends removed
2 tablespoons olive oil
2 tablespoons butter
1 clove garlic, minced
¼ cup minced onion
4 ounces mortadella sausage, diced into ¼-inch cubes
Salt and pepper to taste
1 cup Croutons (garnish) (see following recipe)

1 In large pot, add salt to 5 quarts water. Bring to boil, add beans and cover until water comes to boil again. Uncover and continue to boil 3 minutes, then test beans (they should be tender but still crunchy). Drain immediately in a colander. Unless beans are to be used at once, they should be rinsed under cold running water for 1 minute. (Otherwise steam from cooking water will cause them to lose color.) Cut beans diagonally into 1½-inch lengths.

2 In a large skillet, heat olive oil and butter. Add garlic and onion and sauté until golden.

3 Add string beans to skillet and heat, uncovered, until liquid is absorbed. Add mortadella and heat through. Season to taste with salt and pepper. Place in serving dish and dot with Croutons.

Croutons
Makes 1 cup
¼ cup olive oil
3 slices day-old French bread, trimmed of crusts and cut into ¼-inch cubes

1 Heat olive oil in medium skillet, add bread and sauté until browned on all sides. Drain on paper towels.

*"Guests who have never tasted this before
are delightfully surprised."*

Mozzarella Marinara

¼ **cup seasoned breadcrumbs**
¼ **cup grated Parmesan cheese**
1½ **pounds mozzarella cheese (use brick shape rather than ball)**
2 **eggs, beaten**
¼ **cup all purpose flour**
   Oil (for frying)
2 **cups Pomodoro Sauce (see recipe, page 33) *or* marinara *or* meatless spaghetti sauce**
   Anchovy fillets (optional garnish)

1 Mix together breadcrumbs and Parmesan cheese. Cut mozzarella cheese into pieces 3 inches by 2 inches by ½ inch. Dip pieces in beaten egg, then in flour, then in egg again. Dip into the breadcrumbs and Parmesan, coating completely. *(If cheese slices are not thoroughly coated, cheese will melt into hot oil and stick to pan.)* Chill 30 minutes.

2 Pour oil into large skillet to depth of ½ inch and heat to about 375°F. Add cheese and brown on one side, then turn carefully and brown on other side until the cheese melts, about 3 to 5 minutes.

3 Quickly remove cheese from oil and drain on paper towels. Put a few tablespoons of sauce on individual serving plates, then add the fried mozzarella and another tablespoon of sauce. Garnish each serving with an anchovy fillet. Serve as quickly as possible (cheese will set rapidly as it cools).

" This dish has great success as an appetizer, a side dish, or a light meal."

Spinach-Mushroom Frittata

6 servings

5 tablespoons butter
1 garlic clove, minced
4 scallions, white part only, sliced
½ pound mushrooms, sliced to medium thickness
3 10-ounce packages frozen chopped spinach, thawed and squeezed dry
6 eggs
3 tablespoons whipping cream
1 tablespoon minced fresh parsley
1 teaspoon dried thyme
1 teaspoon dried basil
¾ teaspoon salt
¾ teaspoon pepper
½ cup grated Parmesan cheese
1 tablespoon olive oil (for pan)

1 Melt 4 tablespoons butter in large skillet. Add garlic, scallions and mushrooms and sauté 3 minutes over medium heat. Remove with slotted spoon and drain in colander.

2 Heat 1 tablespoon butter in same skillet and sauté spinach, stirring until liquid has evaporated. Set aside with mushroom mixture.

3 Preheat oven to 375°F. Beat eggs until frothy and add cream, herbs, salt and pepper and ¼ cup Parmesan cheese. Drain vegetables thoroughly and stir into eggs. Pour into 1½- to 2-quart oiled casserole or quiche pan.

4 Bake 20 to 25 minutes. Sprinkle remaining Parmesan on top before serving. If desired, brown top by placing dish under broiler for 1 minute.

*"I've updated only the method in this old
family favorite."*

Onion Torta

8 servings

20 double soda crackers (40 individual squares), crushed

½ cup butter (1 stick), melted, plus 2 tablespoons chilled butter

2½ cups thinly sliced onion

1 cup milk, at boiling point

3 eggs, beaten

¼ teaspoon salt

⅛ teaspoon pepper

½ pound Fontina cheese, shredded

1 Preheat oven to 350°F. Mix cracker crumbs and melted butter and press into bottom and up sides of 9-inch pie pan. Bake 5 minutes.

2 Melt 2 tablespoons chilled butter in medium skillet and sauté onion until soft and golden. Spread onion on bottom of crust.

3 Slowly add milk to eggs, then add salt and pepper and cheese. Mix well.

4 Pour mixture over onion and bake torta until filling is set, 35 to 40 minutes. Allow torta to rest 5 minutes before serving.

"...a heavenly combination of fruit, cream, and chocolate."

Fruit Cioccolata

6 servings
Other fruits may be substituted.

4 **medium navel oranges, peeled, sliced and drained (approximately 3 cups)**
1 **cup sliced strawberries, drained**
3 **bananas, sliced**
1 **cup whipping cream, chilled**
2 **tablespoons sugar**
1 **tablespoon orange liqueur**
1 **cup grated semisweet chocolate**

1 Place oranges, strawberries and bananas in bottom of 9 × 13-inch ovenproof serving dish or ovenproof individual soufflé dishes.

2 Preheat broiler. Whip cream with sugar, add orange liqueur and beat until stiff. Spread whipped cream over fruit.

3 Sprinkle grated chocolate over cream, making sure that no cream remains exposed. (Chocolate layer should be ¼ inch thick.)

4 Place fruit mixture under broiler, 5 inches from heat source. Leave broiler door open. *Watch carefully to avoid burning.* As soon as chocolate is melted and whipped cream shows through, creating a marbled appearance, remove and serve immediately.

"Not only sensational looking, but an easy do-ahead dessert."

Pears in Red Wine

6 servings

2 cups good-quality Chianti
1¼ cups sugar
Juice of 2 lemons
1 cup water
6 pears, peeled, stems intact
1 10-ounce package frozen raspberries, thawed
1 cup whipping cream, chilled
1 teaspoon vanilla

1 In large saucepan, bring to boil the wine, ¾ cup sugar, juice of 1 lemon and water. Lower heat.

2 Remove a slice from bottom of each pear and discard; drop pears into water-wine mixture. Cover and simmer from 20 to 30 minutes, turning carefully a few times. Remove from heat and allow pears to cool in the syrup.

3 In a blender or processor, puree raspberries, remaining ½ cup sugar and juice of second lemon.

4 Remove pears from syrup and drain. Stand pears on end, pour raspberry sauce over them and chill if desired.

5 Whip cream until stiff, then add vanilla. Top pears with whipped cream. Serve cold or at room temperature.

*"A delicious blend of coffee and chocolate
that reminds me of Italy."*

Espresso Mousse

6 servings

4 ounces semisweet chocolate, coarsely chopped

¾ teaspoon instant espresso powder

⅓ cup whipping cream, at boiling point

2 egg yolks

4 egg whites, room temperature

1 cup whipping cream

2 tablespoons confectioner's sugar

½ teaspoon vanilla

1 In blender or processor, blend chocolate and coffee powder at high speed 10 seconds. Add cream and blend for 30 seconds. Scrape down the sides of container and add egg yolks. Blend 15 seconds.

2 In separate bowl, beat egg whites until stiff. Fold chocolate mixture into whites and spoon into serving bowl or individual glasses or serving dishes. Chill until firm.

3 Beat whipping cream until stiff, gradually adding sugar and vanilla. Top mousse with cream and serve.

*"...a nice finish to a rich meal ... light
and uncomplicated."*

Strawberries in Wine

6 servings

1 pint strawberries, hulled
⅓ cup sugar
1 750-ml bottle good-quality
  Chianti
  Juice of 1 lemon

1 Wash strawberries and pat dry; place in large serving bowl.

2 Sprinkle sugar over berries and pour in wine and lemon juice. With a wooden spoon, carefully turn berries over to mix well.

3 Cover bowl and chill for several hours, turning berries once or twice if they are not covered with wine. Serve them with some of the wine in individual bowls or in wine glasses.

" . . . a very festive dessert. I make it for special occasions."

Lemon Spumante

6 servings

½ cup sugar
¼ cup water
2 egg whites, room
   temperature
   Pinch of salt
1 pint lemon sherbet, slightly
   softened
1 teaspoon grated lemon peel
2 tablespoons lemon juice
6 large strawberries (garnish)
   Dry Champagne or Asti
   Spumante, chilled

1 In small saucepan mix sugar and water together. Bring to boil over moderate heat, stirring until sugar is dissolved. Wash down crystals on sides of pan with brush dipped in cold water. Boil syrup without stirring until it reaches soft-ball stage, when a small amount dripped into ice water can be molded into a ball (238°F on a candy themometer). Remove from heat.

2 In mixer, beat egg whites and salt until they form stiff peaks. When syrup is cooked, pour into egg whites in a fine stream while beating constantly at a moderate speed. Beat meringue until it is stiff and cool.

3 Mix softened lemon sherbet with lemon peel and juice. Fold sherbet into meringue. Spoon mixture into stemmed Champagne glasses until ¾ full. Cover with plastic wrap and freeze. (*May be frozen for up to 1 week at this point.*)

4 Remove from freezer 10 minutes before serving. Garnish each serving with strawberry. Pour Champagne or Asti Spumante over each portion to fill glass.

*"As a child, I preferred tortoni to ice cream.
My daughter does, too."*

Almond Biscuit Tortoni

6 to 8 servings

3 tablespoons water
½ cup sugar
2 egg whites, room temperature
⅛ teaspoon salt
8 tablespoons chopped almonds, toasted (toast 12 to 15 minutes at 350°F)
1 cup whipping cream, whipped
1½ teaspoons almond extract

1 In a 1-quart saucepan, heat water with sugar, stirring to dissolve. Boil rapidly without stirring until syrup forms a thread when poured slowly from a teaspoon (236°F on a candy thermometer).

2 While syrup is boiling, beat egg whites with salt until stiff.

3 Pour hot syrup in very thin stream over whites, beating constantly until very stiff peaks form. Cover and refrigerate 30 minutes.

4 Fold in 6 tablespoons almonds, whipped cream and almond extract, reserving 2 tablespoons almonds for garnish. Spoon into 2½-inch foil or paper cups that have been put into a muffin pan. Sprinkle with reserved nuts and freeze. Serve in foil or paper cups.

"I like to add a few strawberries or raspberries for color to this traditional dessert."

Zabaglione

4 egg yolks, room temperature
¼ cup sugar
½ cup dry Marsala
1 cup raspberries or
strawberries (optional)

1 Put yolks and sugar in top of double boiler and whip with a beater or whisk until mixture is pale yellow and thickened.

2 Place container over simmering water in bottom of double boiler. *(Do not permit water to boil.)*

3 Add Marsala slowly to egg mixture and continue beating until soft mounds are formed.

4 Spoon into stemmed glasses over a few berries if desired and serve immediately.

Index

Credits

Photographer: Teri Sandison
Food stylist: Jean E. Carey
Food styling assistant: Sandy Krogh
Jacket and cover design:
    John Brogna
Book design: Paula Schlosser
Recipe tester: Laurel Lyle
Special thanks to: Rose Grant, Mary
    Nadler, and Sylvia Tidwell

The Knapp Press is a wholly owned subsidiary of KNAPP COMMUNICATIONS CORPORATION.
Chairman and Chief Executive Officer: Cleon T. Knapp
President: H. Stephen Cranston
Senior Vice-Presidents: Rosalie Bruno (New Venture Development), Betsy Wood Knapp (Administrative Services/Electronics), Harry Myers (Magazine Group Publisher), William J. N. Porter (Corporate Product Sales), Paige Rense (Editorial), and L. James Wade, Jr. (Finance)

THE KNAPP PRESS

President: Alice Bandy; *Administrative Assistant:* Beth Bell; *Editor:* Norman Kolpas; *Managing Editor:* Pamela Mosher; *Associate Editors:* Colleen Dunn Bates, Jan Koot, Sarah Lifton, Diane Rossen Worthington; *Assistant Editor:* Nancy D. Roberts; *Editorial Assistant:* Teresa Roupe; *Art Director:* Paula Schlosser; *Designer:* Robin Murawski; *Marketing Designer:* Barbara Kosoff; *Book Production Manager:* Larry Cooke; *Book Production Coordinators:* Veronica Losorelli, Joan Valentine; *Director, Rosebud Books:* Robert Groag; *Creative Director, Rosebud Books:* Jeffrey Book; *Financial Manager:* Joseph Goodman; *Assistant Finance Manager:* Kerri Culbertson; *Financial Assistant:* Julie Mason; *Fulfillment Services Manager:* Virginia Parry; *Director of Public Relations:* Jan B. Fox; *Marketing Assistants:* Dolores Briqueleur, Randy Levin; *Promotions Managers:* Joanne Denison, Nina Gerwin; *Special Sales Manager:* Lynn Blocker; *Special Sales Coordinator:* Amy Hershman